Bow Exercises
for the Expressive Violinist

Craddock Road

Bow Exercises for The Expressive Violinist

Copyright

Bow Exercises for The Expressive Violinist

Published by David France Cover art by David France
Author: David France
Editor: Benjamin Schonberg

Copyright © 2025 by David France. All Rights Reserved.

No part of this publication may be reproduced, distributed or transmitted in any form or by any means, including photocopying, recording, or other electronic or mechanical methods, without the prior written permission of the publisher, except in the case of brief quotations embodied in reviews and certain other non-commercial uses permitted by copyright law..

This work is sold with the understanding that neither the author nor the publisher are held responsible for the results accrued from the advice in this book. Printed in the United States of America

First Printing, July 2020
ISBN: 978-0-578-72166-8

Joy in this life is increased when we give our lives away for the joy of others.
-D. France

The Expressive Violinist

Bow control and division are essential elements of a violinist's toolbox for expressive playing. Through careful study, their crowning benefit is the acquisition of an agility in the right hand leading to an ability to play with ease and virtuosity.

The study of these exercises gives the serious student an increased palette of colors, a nuanced amplitude of dynamics, and an increased speed with which new music can be played with beauty and expression.

The ability to play an instrument is a skill to be cherished by individual musicians. It can and should also be enjoyed as a gift that can be used in service towards the happiness and joy of others. The regular practice of bow exercises makes the musician's palette richer thereby increasing their capacity to bring joy to others. This book series is intended as a precursor to the Sevcik Bowing Books.

We hope the technique you gain through the study of this book will make playing the violin easier while bringing joy to yourself and the world around you.

How to Use This Book

The following exercises are intended to separate the practice of bowing patterns and divisions from equally important left hand techniques. For this reason the same finger pattern is used in all exercises on all strings to give the player the opportunity to put their entire focus on developing the art of bowing.

All exercises are to be played on a single string. The fourth finger should be used in all exercises to allow for the attention to be placed on bow divisions on a single string. Part 3 of this series covers foundational string crossing exercises and Part 1 is a thorough study of how to build an Expressive Bow Arm from the beginning of one's study of the violin.

We encourage you to practice the book in the order presented but teachers, students, and professionals should feel free to choose the sequence that fits best with their own philosophies of the development of bow facility.

The exercises should be practiced daily with a metronome to promote an even bow speed in the various parts of the bow. The advanced student and professional are encouraged to gradually use slower speeds for the acquisition of greater bow control and the attainment of a richer sound.

Points of Practice

- Memorize each exercise and *practice in front of the mirror*, watching the bow to keep it parallel to the bridge.

- Each Exercise in this book is to be played with an Up Bow upon repeating the exercise.

- The First time through the book familiarize yourself with the exercises by practicing each exercise on a single string through the entire book. The 2nd time through the book practice all the exercises on all strings. Each time thereafter use the index of bowing patterns and change the string as you desire.

- If keeping the bow straight is your primary focus, remain on Exercise #1 for the number of days, weeks, or months it might take you to play consistently with a bow that is parallel to the bridge.

- Play each exercise with all the hairs of the bow placed flatly on the string.

- Exercises played near the frog or the tip should be played to the extreme ends of the bow. In the beginning of study you will improve faster if you sometimes get so far to the tip the bow falls off the string or you play so close to the frog that you hit the metal. If over time you pay close attention to listening to the quality of the sound in every part of the bow, making weight, speed, and placement adjustments as necessary, you will develop the ability to play with the entire bow with a clean and consistent sound.

Bow Division

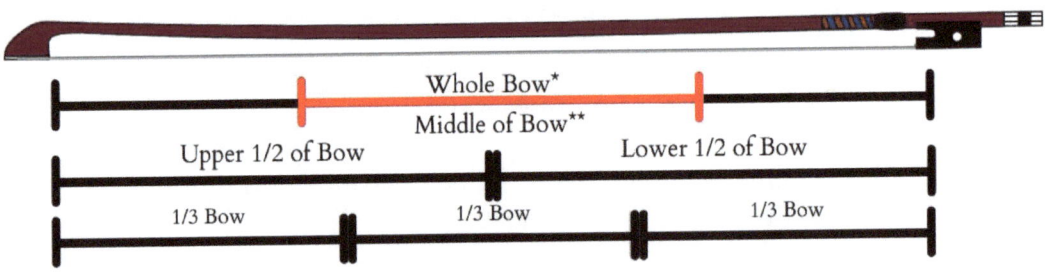

*Whole Bow includes the entire length of the bow from the tip to the frog
**Middle of Bow includes only the secction in red

7

2. Four Staccato Notes (with Fingerings)

to be played in the middle of the bow

A-string

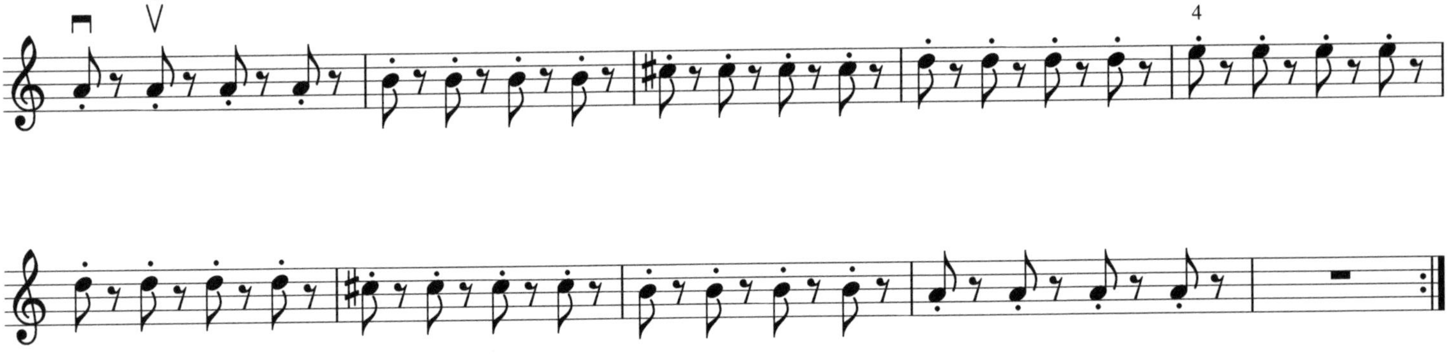

D-string

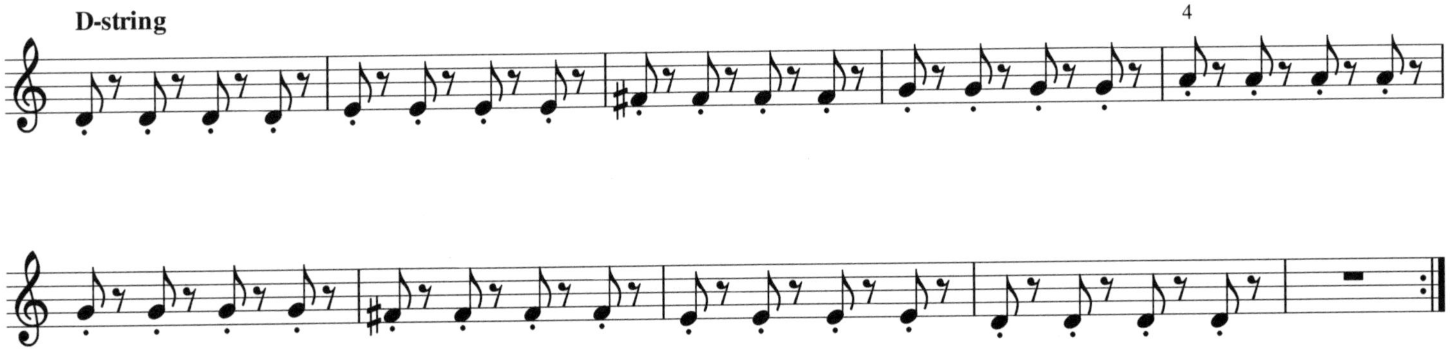

E-string

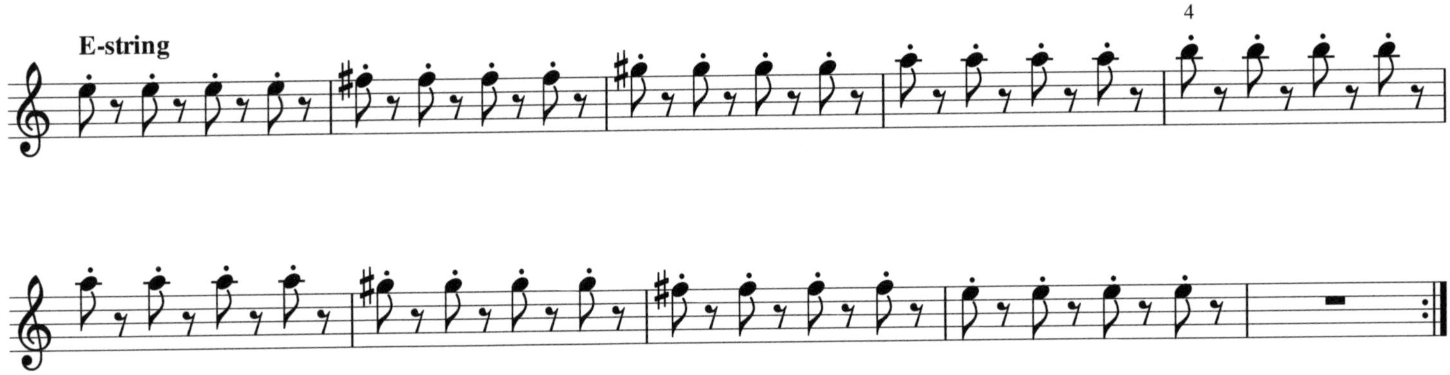

G-string

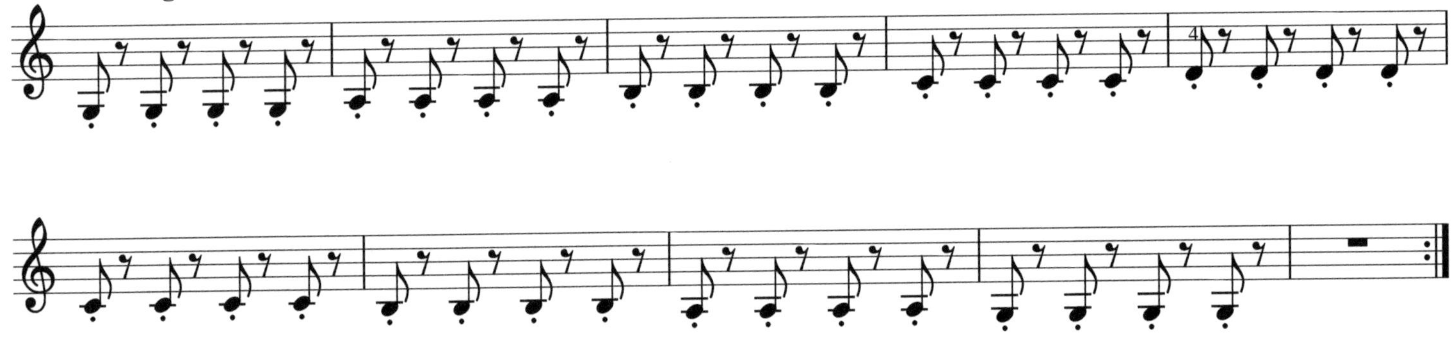

3. Detaché
to be played in each third of the bow

A-string

D-string

E-string

G-string

4. Whole Bow (Half Notes)
each note is to be played with the entire bow

A-string

D-string

E-string

G-string

5. Martelé *
to be played in the lower half of the bow

A-string

D-string

E-string

G-string
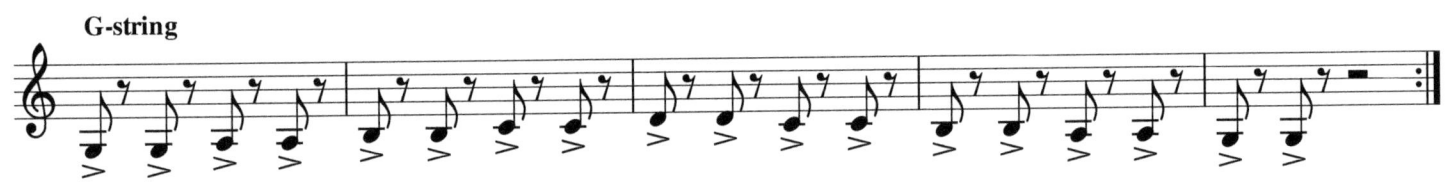

* advanced players can further develop balance and control by playing this exercise at times without the pinky on the bow

6. Whole Bow (Whole Notes)

A-string

D-string
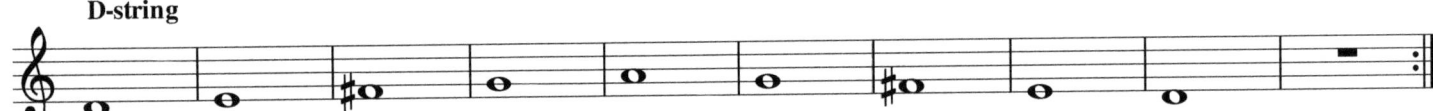

E-string
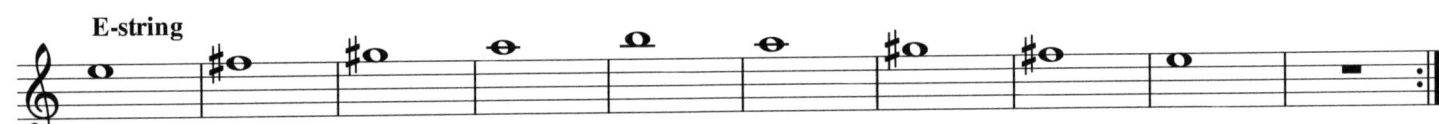

G-string
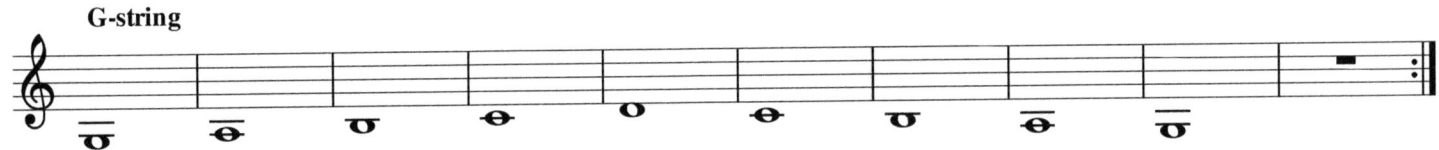

7. Whole and Half Bow
half notes to be played with the whole bow,
quarter notes to be played with a half bow

A-string

D-string

E-string

G-string

8. Slurred Notes
slurred notes to be played with the whole bow,
separate notes to be played with a half bow*

A-string

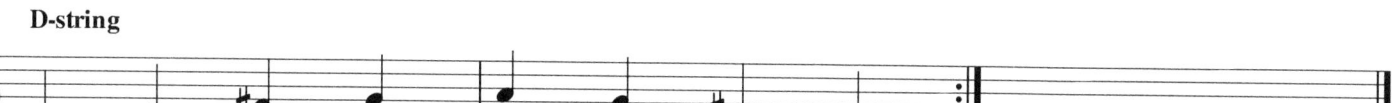

D-string

E-string

G-string

*observe that the bowing here is the same as the bowing in 7.

9. Martelé
to be played in the upper half of the bow

A-string

D-string

E-string

G-string

10. A Third of the Bow and a Whole Bow
eighth notes to be played with a third of the bow,
half notes to be played with a whole bow

A-string

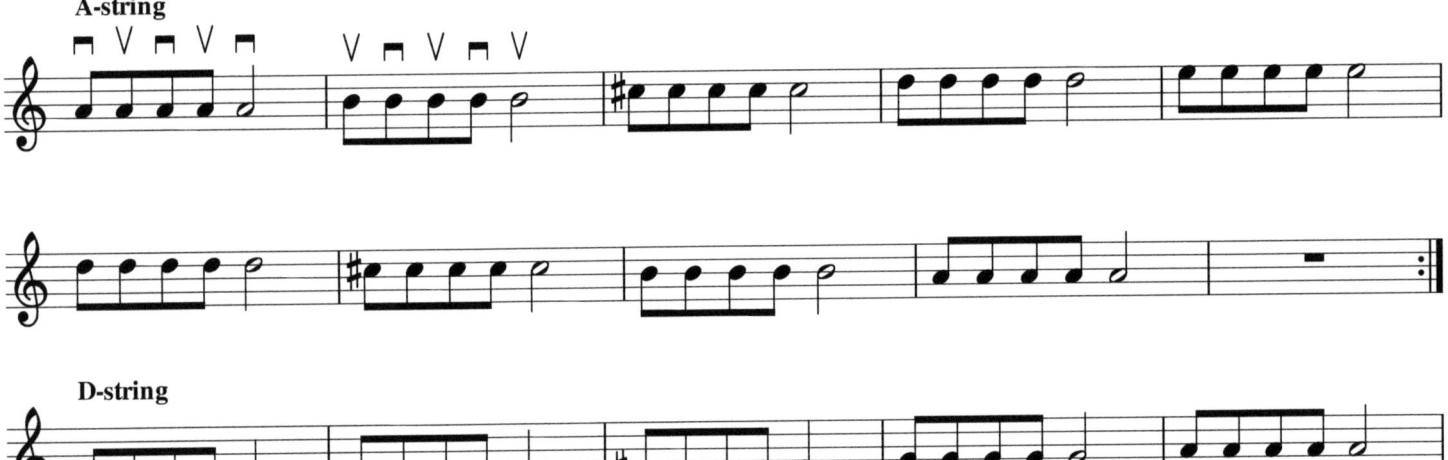

D-string

11. More Slurred Notes
each set of slurred notes to be played with the whole bow*

*the bowing here is the same as the bowing from 4.

12. Hooked Bow
to be distributed equally over the entire bow

A-string

D-string

E-string

G-string

13. Up/Down-bow Staccato
to be distributed equally over the entire bow,
the exercise is also beneficial over each half and each third of the bow

A-string

D-string

14. Collé
to be played at the middle, tip, and frog

David France is a Graduate of the New England Conservatory of Music and has an honorary Doctorate from Champlain College in Vermont. He is a champion for helping others take their first steps toward their lifelong dreams.

He is an enthusiastic pedagogue and is the author of *Bow Exercises for the Expressive Violinist, Bow Exercises for the Expressive String Orchestra,* and the Best-Seller *Show Up:, Unlocking the Power of Relational Networking.*

He has taught at the St. Joseph School of Music, The St. Paul Conservatory of Music, and the Bermuda School of Music. He has given masterclasses internationally in Mexico, Costa Rica, Scotland, India, and Venezuela and has guest lectured at Harvard, MIT, Yale, and the New England Conservatory of Music.

He was the winner of the international competition that formed the first YouTube Symphony and served as one of its Concertmasters. He also was named one of the Top 40 Urban Innovators under 40 in the United States for his work with inner city youth in Boston. He has performed with Quincy Jones, John Legend, Smokey Robinson, Kenny Rogers along with The Wichita Symphony, Minnesota Orchestra, and the Sphinx Symphony.

He has appeared on the NBC Nightly News, BBC News, Al Jazeera English as well as in Time Magazine, the Washington Post, among many other publications. He has been featured in documentaries, reality shows, and has recorded on soundtracks for numerous films.

A committed advocate for students, his former students have performed at Carnegie Hall and Lincoln Center and have attended the University of Minnesota, Berklee college of Music, and the Curtis Institute of Music in Philadelphia. They have also won numerous awards including the grand prize in the Youth Division of the Sphinx Strings Competition in Detroit. In his first 7 years teaching in Bermuda he taught over 400 students how to play the violin at the Bermuda School of Music and at satellite programs at Purvis, Victor Scott, and Francis Patton Primary Schools.

His teachers include a roster of the most internationally recognized teachers of the violin & violin including Sally O'Reilly, Roland and Almita Vamos, and Aaron Janse.

He is an avid traveler and believes Joy in Life is increased when you give your life away for the Joy of others.

Notes

Use the following pages to take notes on details of how to practice each exercise

Notes

Use the following pages to take notes on details of how to practice each exercise

Notes

Use the following pages to take notes on details of how to practice each exercise

Notes

Use the following pages to take notes on details of how to practice each exercise

Notes

Use the following pages to take notes on details of how to practice each exercise

Notes

Use the following pages to take notes on details of how to practice each exercise

Notes

Use the following pages to take notes on details of how to practice each exercise

Notes

Use the following pages to take notes on details of how to practice each exercise